E is for the Eras Tour

Now I Know My Tay-B-C's

Dear Swiftie,

I sat down and made this book for my sweet Hadley, and it contains elements that remind us of our favorite musical genius!

Whether you were able to attend the Eras tour in person, or you were blessed by a live stream, I hope you enjoy this book for years to come.

xoxo,
Jessica Armstrong

a fellow Swiftie

is for All Too Well

The ten minute version of course

is for Bad Blood

She's Fine. She wasn't doing anything. Hey! Stop!

is for Cruel Summer

is for Dear John

is for Enchanted

is for Fearless

is for Getaway Car

is for Hits Different

is for Invisible String

is for July 7th

is for Karma

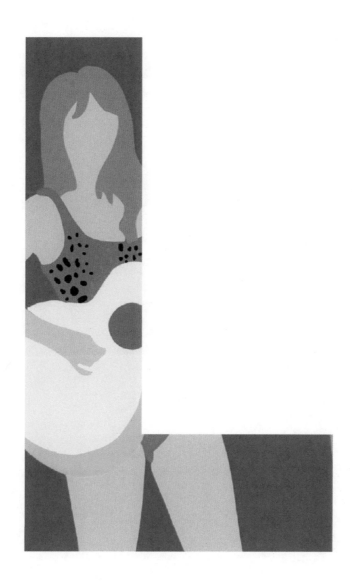

is for Lover

is for Marjorie & Mama Swift

is for Nothing New

is for Our Song

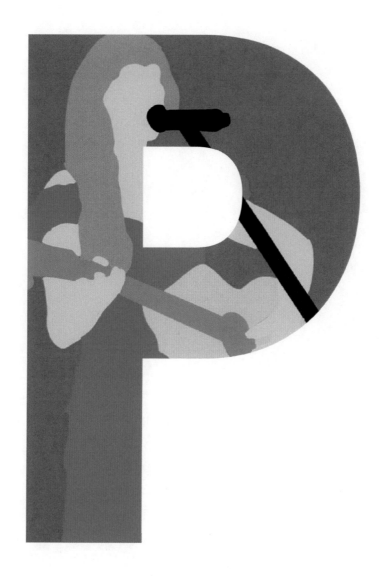

is for Paper Rings

is for Question

is for Ready for It

is for Style

is for Taylor's Version

The only version we listen to

is for Umbrella

is for Vigilante

is for Willow

is for XL Blue Crewneck

is for You're On Your Own, Kid

is for Zero regrets for being a Swiftie

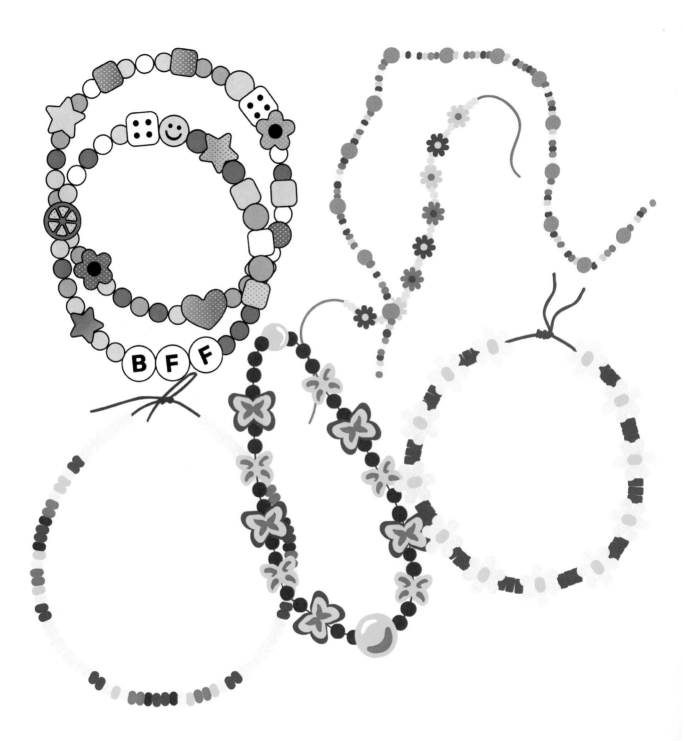

A few friendship bracelets from us to you!